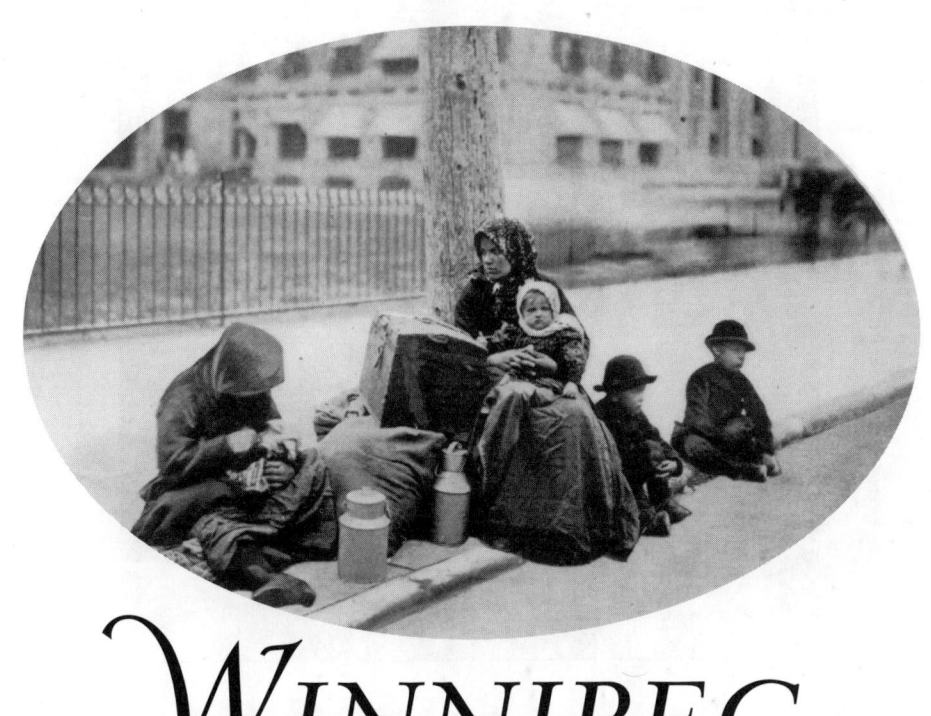

WINNIPEG

Monument commemorating the Seven Oaks Massacre of 1816 (West Kildonan).

Provincial Archives of Manitoba - Foote Collection - N2050

(Previous page)
Immigrant family of five, women in babushkas, sitting on the street in front of the CPR station (1905).

Provincial Archives of Manitoba - Immigration Collection - N7935

GLIMPSES OF THE WAY WE WERE

A WINNIPEG *Album*

John David Hamilton & Bonnie Dickie

HOUNSLOW PRESS
A MEMBER OF THE DUNDURN GROUP
TORONTO · OXFORD

Copyright © John David Hamilton and Bonnie Dickie 1998

All rights reserved. No part of this publication may be reproduced, stored in a retrieval system, or transmitted in any form or by any means, electronic, mechanical, photocopying, recording, or otherwise (except for brief passages for purposes of review) without the prior permission of Hounslow Press. Permission to photocopy should be requested from the Canadian Reprography Collective.

Publisher: Anthony Hawke
Editor: Barry Jowett
Design: John Lee
Printer: Transcontinental Printing Inc.

Canadian Cataloguing in Publication Data

Hamilton, John David, 1919-
A Winnipeg album: glimpses of the way we were

ISBN 0-88882-204-9
1. Winnipeg (Man.) — History — Pictorial works. I. Dickie, Bonnie. II. Title

FC3396.37.H36 1998   971.27'43'00222   C98-931585-1
F1064.5.W7H34 1998

1   2   3   4   5   02   01   00   99   98

We acknowledge the support of the **Canada Council for the Arts** for our publishing program. We also acknowledge the support of the **Ontario Arts Council** and the **Book Publishing Industry Development Program** of the **Department of Canadian Heritage**.

Care has been taken to trace the ownership of copyright material used in this book. The author and the publisher welcome any information enabling them to rectify any references or credit in subsequent editions.

Printed and bound in Canada.

Printed on recycled paper.

Hounslow Press	Hounslow Press	Hounslow Press
8 Market Street	73 Lime Walk	2250 Military Road
Suite 200	Headington, Oxford,	Tonawanda NY
Toronto, Canada	England	U.S.A. 14150
M5E 1M6	OX3 7AD	

Lower Fort Garry (1878).

PAM - Fort Garry Collection - N1033

Louis Riel, just after the 1898 rebellion.

PAM - Riel Collection - N5771

Riel hanged in effigy in Winnipeg (1885).

PAM - Events Collection - N9582

Here is what the city became in 1950!

PAM - Winnipeg Views Collection - N8438

Winnipeg

"...why, Winnipeg is the REAL Camelot! Built faster than the original and never collapsed either!"
— *son of a Manitoba pioneer.*

Glimpses of the Way We Were

INTRODUCTION

1881 WAS THE YEAR of the showdown at the OK Corral in Tombstone, Arizona, and the year when Sitting Bull returned to the United States after five years sanctuary in Canada following the Battle of the Little Big Horn.

More important, it was the year of the Winnipeg railroad boom when Canadians seriously began building the CPR and settling the prairies. In many ways, Winnipeg was the most turbulent town on a wild frontier because it was the single gateway to the Canadian West — the only comparable American entrance ports were Kansas City and St. Joseph, Missouri. Winnipeg prepared the way for Regina, Saskatoon, Edmonton, Calgary ... even far-off Vancouver. This was Camelot, one of a hundred Camelot's about to rise on the prairies between the North Saskatchewan River and the Rio Grande, and the Red River of the north and the Red River of the south.

It was a time of rugged frontiersmen whether they were aboriginal Indians, Metis buffalo hunters, or navvies on the railroad.

Winnipeg had as much colour as Kansas City, Denver, or Omaha, and in our own history it was more important than any of these cities were in the development of the United States.

But what made Winnipeg and its North American counterparts different was that the prairies were opened at the time of the greatest technological revolution in the history of mankind, which saw the emergence of railway and steamboat travel, the telegraph, the telephone, the electric light bulb and the electric motor, the internal combustion engine, and the airplane.

The Red River Rebellion came in 1869, before the Selkirk Settlement at the Forks of the Red and Assiniboine had established a real town. There were a few settlers and a few long-sighted hustlers who saw possibilities in the future and were determined to steal a stake from the Indians and Metis. Their prototype was Dr. John Schultz, villain or hero, who fought Riel and ended up a knight and lieutenant-governor of the province. Manitoba was already a part of the new nation of Canada when Crazy Horse killed Custer in 1876.

The CPR set up shop in Winnipeg in 1881, and from then on the city's future was mapped out.

As for my family, my grandfather, Dave Hamilton, a gawky, twenty-two-year-old Ontario farm boy, came to Winnipeg first in 1881. He said there were 100,000 people when he arrived and only 10,000 when he came back during the bust a few years later. Both were exaggerated figures, but he had already embraced the big brag fashion of the west. My father, at 13, lived in a "soddy" on the bald prairie in 1900 while the homestead house was being built. I was conceived on a bush cattle ranch north of Winnipeg in 1919.

So my western ties go as deep as any white man's, apart from the French-Canadian voyageurs and the Selkirk Settlers.

Winnipeg

Wagons at Portage and Main — before there was a city to go with them (1872).

PAM - Winnipeg Streets Collection - N5774

Glimpses of the Way We Were

American covered wagons heading west — in Canada (1880).

PAM - Immigration Collection - N7933

WINNIPEG

The village grows (1874).

PAM - Stovel Advocate Collection - N10213

Glimpses of the Way We Were

Parking was easy on Main Street (1883) ...

PAM - Transportation Collection - N1424

WINNIPEG

... but there were crowds at times.

PAM - Winnipeg Buildings Collection - N4450

Glimpses of the Way We Were

The family station wagon — an Indian family with a Red River cart.

PAM - Transportation Collection — N1428

13

WINNIPEG

Or you might prefer the latest 1880s model of a skidoo. (Dog teams in front of The Hudson's Bay Company).

PAM - Winnipeg Buildings Collection - N9724

Glimpses of the Way We Were

The settlement at The Forks began in violence with the Seven Oaks Massacre in 1816, when Nor'Wester buffalo hunters struck down Scottish settlers and continued with the first Riel rebellion in 1869. This was rough frontier country. The crooks and hustlers from Upper Canada had been stealing land from Metis settlers for a generation with the full support of the Queen's government, and the Metis were finally lashing back. Louis Riel was hanged for his pains. His antagonist during the rebellion, Dr. John Schultz, lived on to become a knight of the realm and lieutenant-governor of Manitoba.

Apart from the rebellion, the transition from frontier fur-trading post to real city went with remarkable speed and efficiency. Winnipeg grew up at the Forks of the Assiniboine and Red — which became the corner of Portage and Main — while Riel's home town of St. Boniface, across the Red, became a peaceful village, then a town.

Winnipeg

Bakery in 1900 on what would become Tache Boulevard.

PAM - St. Boniface Streets Collection - N9368

Glimpses of the Way We Were

Norwood Hotel.

PAM - St. Boniface Streets
Collection - N9374

17

Winnipeg

Whether you were laying out a lawn or turning the sod for the Red River railway to the States, that awful gumbo mud had to be dealt with.

PAM - Events Collection - N8942

Glimpses of the Way We Were

More and more branch lines spread out — to the American border and to Hudson Bay.

PAM - Transportation Collection - 25

Winnipeg

As soon as the railways arrived, farmers hitched up the old ox to the wagon and unloaded supplies.

PAM - Immigration Collection - N7934

Glimpses of the Way We Were

The immigrants never stopped coming, and in 1915 they were surging in almost as fast as in 1910.

PAM - Foote Collection - N2066

Winnipeg

By 1910, the CPR was a venerable institution and ready to make a monument of the first locomotive, the Countess of Dufferin, *before an enthusiastic crowd.*

PAM - Transportation Collection - N17

Glimpses of the Way We Were

As the new postage-stamp province of Manitoba began to fill up, the settlers brought with them civilization on every level. Among the first institutions were the churches, which began as missions but soon took on a much more important role. The Roman Catholics and Anglicans had missions and schools in 1820; the Presbyterians came in the 1870s and the Methodists in the 1880s. For many years, Wesley College was the only high school in Manitoba.

Manitoba College (Presbyterian).

PAM - Foote Collection - N2694

23

Winnipeg

St. Boniface College, Bishop's Palace, and Cathederal.

PAM - St. Boniface Collection - N9360

Glimpses of the Way We Were

New St. Boniface Roman Catholic Cathedral.

PAM - St. Boniface Collection - N11893

Winnipeg

St. John's College (Anglican).

PAM - Foote Collection - N2685

Glimpses of the Way We Were

Wesley College (Methodist).

PAM - Winnipeg Views Collection — N11801

Winnipeg

WESLEY COLLEGE was unique among the religious institutions of higher learning on the prairies. The Roman Catholics, Anglicans, and Presbyterians all sent their clergy out to minister unto the aboriginals and the newcomers and their colleges were largely used at first to train missionaries. But the Methodists had a broader perspective. For many years, Wesley College was the only high school in the province and it also threw open its doors to young people of all denominations. Until the Second World War at least, the non-sectarian University of Manitoba was segregated and had a quota system which kept out most Jews. It was also too expensive for poor immigrant boys and girls and its president, Sydney Smith, said publicly that only the well-to-do should be given a higher education.

But Wesley College, under Principal J.H. Riddell, welcomed everybody and kept its fees low. That meant there were many students who were the sons and daughters of impoverished clergymen and school teachers. But there were many Jews, Ukrainians, and other Central and Eastern Europeans, and even Canadian Indians.

We learned about one another and Wesley became perhaps the greatest force for tolerance in a province that had always been riven by religious and racial bigotry.

I am eternally grateful to my alma mater.

Religion came to the prairies with the La Verendryes, who built Fort Maurepas in 1734 near the Forks where the Assiniboine River joined the Red. This had been one of the great junction points of the world from time immemorial: here woodland and plains' Indians met to trade — down the Red from the south, east along the Assiniboine from the true prairies, west along the Winnipeg River from the east, up the Red from Lake Winnipeg and the whole Saskatchewan River system.

Roman Catholic missionaries were at the Forks early and they were soon followed by Anglican and Presbyterian missionaries. As elsewhere, religion was a two-edged sword as far as the aboriginals were concerned. On the one hand, the missionaries tried to moderate the behaviour of the more rapacious white traders while at the same time bringing Christianity to the natives. On the other hand, Christian missionaries did their best to wipe out native religions and, indeed, all native culture.

Later, the Christian clergymen and Jewish rabbis were a pervasive influence on the new white settlers who poured in with the building of the railroads.

The early city of Winnipeg grew up around tiny Central Park, which in turn was close to several impressive churches, such as Knox Presbyterian.

Glimpses of the Way We Were

Knox Church (Presbyterian).

PAM - Foote Collection - N2400

The Rich

THIS AREA was half a mile or so inland from the Forks and close to the commercial district. The early merchants and entrepreneurs built their first houses on both sides of Portage Avenue and south to Broadway. But as they grew rich, they started building mansions.

Broadway, paralleling Portage Avenue, was marked out as a centre of elegance — a broad boulevard fringed with planted trees. It was the place for the legislature, the law courts, the university, impressive stone churches, and the first mansions.

By 1900, the richest man in Winnipeg, J.A. Ashdown, had built his mansion on Broadway. He was the hardware prince who supplied the whole west and soon was to become the mayor and a crony of premiers.

Winnipeg

Broadway from on high (1910).

PAM - Winnipeg Streets Collection - N4571

Glimpses of the Way We Were

Ashdown Mansion on Broadway (1900).

PAM - Winnipeg Streets Collection - N4561PAM -

Winnipeg

But very soon the rich began to feel that Broadway was too close to business, to the great unwashed mass of immigrants. The millionaires moved to the shady and protected bends of the Assiniboine's south bank, well away from the bustling multitudes. The new home of Winnipeg's rich was Roslyn Road and Wellington Crescent, which became the very symbols of luxury and superiority.

Douglas C. Cameron's house on Roslyn Road.

PAM - Winnipeg Homes Collection - N15529

Glimpses of the Way We Were

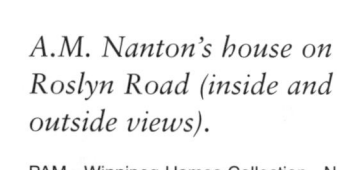

A.M. Nanton's house on Roslyn Road (inside and outside views).

PAM - Winnipeg Homes Collection - N15399 & N15396

Winnipeg

R.H. Hayward's house on St. Mary Avenue.

PAM - Winnipeg Homes Collection - N16622

Glimpses of the Way We Were

Throughout a period of change in the city of Winnipeg, elegance was maintained by the rich and privileged, who were glad to welcome British aristocracy. For example, what more fashionable figures than the following:

Two elegant ladies (1890).

PAM - Costumes Collection - N17777

Winnipeg

Lord Baden Powell inspects Winnipeg Scouts (1910).

PAM - Foote Collection - N1738

Glimpses of the Way We Were

Governor General Earl Grey, Lieutenant-Governor D.H. McMillan, and their ladies.

PAM - Foote Collection - N2037

Winnipeg

Governor General Baron Byng of Vimy, Lieutenant-Governor J.A.M. Aikins, and their entourage (1922).

PAM - Foote Collection - N1759

Glimpses of the Way We Were

Wedding party at train.

PAM - Foote Collection - N15817

Winnipeg

O N THE OTHER SIDE of Winnipeg there were always the poor. The false fronts, flimsy stores, and warehouses and hotels were soon displaced by solid brick and stone structures, but the originals remained as flophouses for the down-and-out, cheap stores for the immigrant thousands, and shack residences for impoverished families.

New York's Lower East Side and London's East End were certainly no worse than the worst of Winnipeg's immigrant slums where Slavs, Italians, Scandinavians, Germans, Jews, a few blacks, and a few Chinese huddled in misery. Winnipeg's special addition to this level of hell was the cold. The only thing that could be said in favour of the Canadian experience was that most of these people would soon move on to farms and small towns where they would have a better chance of improving their lot. And thousands managed to get jobs in Winnipeg itself and to build modest but acceptable homes in the residential districts of the west end or Fort Rouge.

Glimpses of the Way We Were

Immigrants in slums, in what was known as "New Jerusalem" (1904).

PAM - Winnipeg Streets Collection - N796

Winnipeg

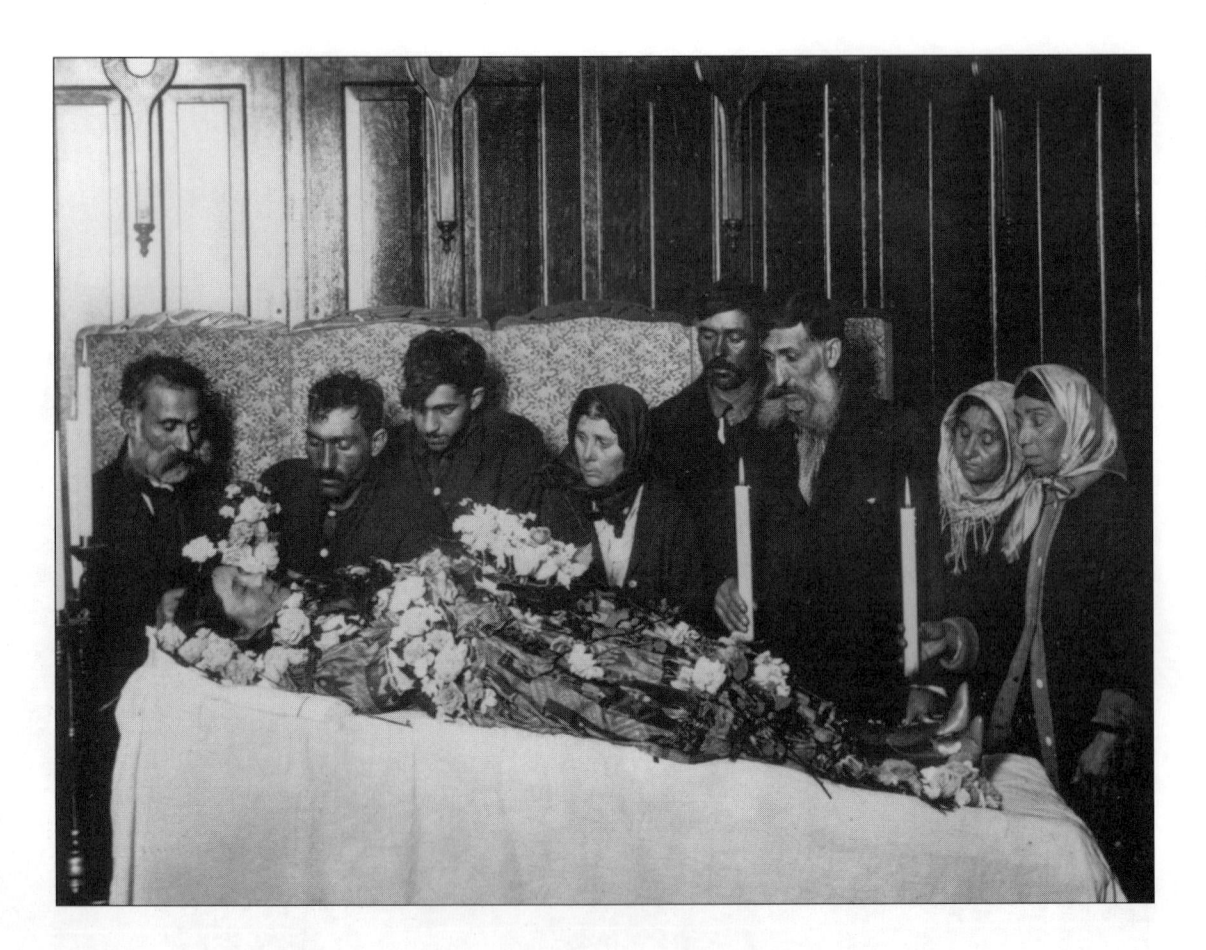

Gypsy funeral.

PAM - Foote Collection - N1728

Glimpses of the Way We Were

"The Foreign Section."

PAM - Immigration Collection - N7938

Winnipeg

An early institution: Drewery's Brewery (1882).

PAM - Winnipeg Buildings
Collection - N16511

Glimpses of the Way We Were

"Older" Main Street (1921).

PAM - Foote Collection - N2701

Winnipeg

"Old" Main Street (1928).

PAM - Winnipeg Streets Collection - N2696

Glimpses of the Way We Were

Part of Winnipeg's early town planning involved the entertainment of the hordes of newcomers who came flooding out of the CPR station looking for "fun, booze, and broads" on Main Street. Saloons sprang up everywhere, and the grifters supplied games of chance where the immigrants and farm workers could lose their pay. No women were allowed in the saloons, but thousands of males bellied up to the bar for rotgut and beer.

Prostitution was another matter: it was as old as the city — at first being practised in shacks and tents near the corner of Portage and Main — then moved a mile or so west on Portage Avenue. As respectable families began building in west central Winnipeg, so began a howl of outrage against the working girls. Finally, the police tried to restrict prostitution to an area with fewer respectable citizens to complain. They found it east of the CPR station in a loop of the Red River called Point Douglas.

Point Douglas before the hookers (1900).

PAM - Winnipeg Views Collection - N4551

Winnipeg

THE GAS WORKS filled the area between the CPR station and Annabella, where there were houses on one side and gas works on the other. The adjoining McFarlane Street was an extension of the red-light area. The prostitutes were encouraged to buy the flimsy, two-storey wooden houses in the area and move in. Soon the police chief and the city fathers made it a true red-light district of permitted sex (though not bootlegging). Hundreds of girls moved into the famous Annabella area. The more "respectable" madams had a classy clientele and filled their parlours with plush furniture and gilded knick-knacks. The only raids were for liquor violations, and some brothels became famous for their prominent customers. Winnipeg had its own Storyville and one *Free Press* reporter recalled covering a sudden death in an Annabella Street brothel in 1940. A woman approached the investigating police and told them the victim had died of a heart attack. Asked to tell more she said plaintively: "This guy comes in and we go at it. He likes it and asks for seconds, then thirds. Right in the middle of the third time he croaks. Now I want to know who is going to pay me my six bucks?"

Of course, that was a story that did not appear in either the *Free Press* or the *Tribune!*

Unlike other North American police, who seemed to be mainly Irish, the Winnipeg force was made up of Scots. They were a brawny lot.

Police constable in fur coat and hat. This beat cop was photographed in 1892, but his grandchildren were patrolling Winnipeg streets half a century later — and in similar winter uniforms.

PAM - Winnipeg Police Department Collection - 8

Glimpses of the Way We Were

"Stalwart" was the word for Winnipeg police, whether one was talking about the men themselves or their police stations.

The Force in front of the James Avenue station (1886).

PAM - Winnipeg Police Department
Collection - N11699

Winnipeg

ONE CAN SEE the similarities between 1886 and 1910 with the detective force taking in a couple of murder suspects.

"Winnipeg's Finest" with two young murder suspects.

PAM - Foote Collection - N2651

Glimpses of the Way We Were

And the city had safe-blowers, too ...

PAM - Foote Collection - N2651

Winnipeg

Perpetrators ended up in the handsome law courts on Broadway and the Vaughan Street jail.

The law courts on Broadway (1923).

PAM - Winnipeg Buildings Collection - 19

Glimpses of the Way We Were

The Vaughan Street Jail (1912).

PAM - Winnipeg Buildings Collection

Winnipeg

For many years, executions were staged in the Vaughan Street Jail yard, and black canvas canopies were draped around it to hide the gallows from pedestrians walking past. As a small boy I was told that hangings were held on the grounds of the legislative buildings on Broadway, and I had a persistent vision of a great black square hiding a gallows from me. Indeed, I was sure that the infamous serial murderer of the 1920s, Earl Nelson, "the Strangler," was executed on the legislative grounds almost before my eyes. But my childish imagination was inaccurate: the early executions took place a few blocks away at the jail, and even those ceased when the jail was moved to the suburb of Headingly. When I was a sports writer on the *Free Press*, the night city editor assigned a young and innocent cub reporter to cover an execution that was to occur at Headingly at midnight. When he came back I saw him typing away industriously and asked him about it. He looked at me with ingenuous blue eyes and replied:

"Gee, it was a swell party! Eats and everything!"

Such was the vulgar, bad-taste standard of newspapermen two generations ago.

Glimpses of the Way We Were

It was a crude world we grew up in, and it was surprising that we got relatively civilized as fast as we did. This was attributed to our clergymen and school teachers rather than our politicians. The mighty financial institutions supplied a measure of stability.

Above all, the Grain Exchange and other financial neighbours like the Great West Life Assurance Company and the Royal Trust, formed the focus of Winnipeg. The Grain Exchange was in operation as early as the 1880s and it was the biggest one west of Chicago ...

Winnipeg

External view of Grain Exchange on Lombard Street.

PAM - Winnipeg Streets Collection - N1434

Glimpses of the Way We Were

Interior of the Grain Exchange with the Bulls and Bears at play.

PAM - N9874

57

Winnipeg

OTHER POWER was exemplified by the CPR, its railway station, and the first western locomotive, the *Countess of Dufferin*. The *Countess*, incidentally, was built specifically for the prairies, but arrived by boat before the rails were laid — it served valiantly for more than twenty odd years. Finally, it became a monument displayed in front of the CPR station in 1910.

The CPR station in 1939, decorated for the Royal Visit.

PAM - Foote Collection - N2662

Glimpses of the Way We Were

THE CNR arrived later, but it was equally impressive.

The CNR station.

PAM - Winnipeg Views Collection - N8378

Winnipeg

An earlier force in the area was the Hudson's Bay Company, here represented by the Upper Fort Garry Gate, with the visiting Buffalo Bill Wild West Show posing in front in 1910 ...

Upper Fort Garry Gate.

PAM - Fort Garry Collection - N10773

Glimpses of the Way We Were

... and the HBC department store (left) with the magnificent legislative buildings in the background (centre) ...

HBC Store on Memorial Boulevard.

PAM - Winnipeg Streets Collection - N18069

Winnipeg

... and the great wholesale and retail hardware empire of James Ashdown, which built the whole west.

Ashdown's store on Main Street.

PAM - Thomas Burns Collection - 626

Glimpses of the Way We Were

SUCH WERE the power bases on which Winnipeg was built. But when it got down to it, the ordinary, hardworking citizen was the true strength of the city. As late as 1923, Mr. Good Citizen was being supplied with his fuel by endless lines of horse-drawn woodsleds. And when he moved his house he employed more horses.

Woodsleds in winter.

PAM - Foote Collection - N2015

Winnipeg

House-moving.

PAM - Foote Collection - N2474

Glimpses of the Way We Were

EVERYTHING WAS being done in a rush from 1880 or so until the Great Depression started in the 1930s. Farmers came together by train to compare notes and the Manitoba Agricultural College became internationally famous for developing fast-ripening strains of wheat suitable for the short season and early frosts on the prairies. The rush of immigrants peaked in 1914, stopped during the Great War, then exploded once more in the 1920s as thousands escaped from the battlefields of Europe.

Agricultural College get-together.

PAM - Transportation Collection - N9231

WINNIPEG

More immigrants in 1927!

PAM - Foote Collection - N2066

Glimpses of the Way We Were

THE MAGIC that made Winnipeg into a combination of Camelot and Oz was the electric street railway — it truly revolutionized the building of all western North American cities and sped up the process beyond all belief. The first electric railway was tried out in 1888 in Pennsylvania, and by 1892 it had reached Winnipeg. Because it was cheap to build (compared to regular railroads) and in Winnipeg's case could draw on economical hydro-electric power, the street railway turned decades into months.

The technique was simple: run a trolley line out along the existing main trails far into the country, then sell housing lots all the way to the end. There were three main lines in Winnipeg, all starting from the corner of Portage and Main: one went south along the old Pembina Trail; one went north along the Red; the third followed the Portage Trail west along the Assiniboine. As a lure, the city fathers built Assiniboine Park on the south side of the Assiniboine River at the end of Portage Avenue, with a footbridge linking it to the avenue but no vehicle road. Kildonan Park, near the old Selkirk Settlement, was at the north end of Main Street, and River Park was on the Pembina Trail beside the Red. Now a factory or office worker could build a modest family home well out in the country and still get to his job cheaply and speedily.

The historic day in 1892 when the trolley car went into service was captured on film and the growth of the city could be traced through its traffic growth in the early years:

Winnipeg

Trolleys replace horse-drawn street cars (1892).

PAM - Transportation Collection - N7600

Glimpses of the Way We Were

Looking north on Main Street (1894).

PAM - Winnipeg Streets Collection - N9799

Winnipeg

Portage Avenue. The Eaton's Store is on the right in the foreground; the Grain Exchange in the distance in the centre of the picture (1912).

PAM - Winnipeg Streets Collection - N14380

Glimpses of the Way We Were

No cars yet; only bicycles, wagons, and trolleys (1900).

PAM - Winnipeg Streets Collection - N17275

Winnipeg

The best in gingerbread castles: City Hall in 1886.

PAM - Winnipeg Buildings Collection - N9088

Glimpses of the Way We Were

The business area grows.

PAM - Winnipeg Streets Collection - N17275

Winnipeg

Each owner was his own architect, as these differing styles suggest.

PAM - Winnipeg Streets Collection - 1

Glimpses of the Way We Were

Talk about traffic jams!

PAM - Winnipeg Streets Collection - N7968

Winnipeg

And they got worse!

PAM - Winnipeg Streets Collection - N10342

Glimpses of the Way We Were

Except now and then ...

PAM - Winnipeg Streets Collection - N1092

Winnipeg

Or you could sunbathe in Market Square back of City Hall.

PAM - Winnipeg Buildings Collection - N4722

Glimpses of the Way We Were

THE CAMERA recorded proof of the total triumph of the electric trolley as a city builder. There were few automobiles, but the wonderful parks were jammed with pedestrians who travelled for a while on a street car to get to an office picnic, a church gathering, or a family event.

The footbridge to Assiniboine Park.

PAM - Foote Collection - N2258

Winnipeg

The excursion boat Winnitoba *on the Red River at Lockport, north of the city.*

PAM - Foote Collection - N2549

Glimpses of the Way We Were

Hudson's Bay Company annual picnic in 1910.

PAM - Transportation Collection - N3706

81

Winnipeg

From the time that Sir George Simpson ruled his Red River barony in colonial grandeur from Lower Fort Garry, the head men dreamed of dignity and respect. The early provincial legislature on Broadway had its own charm ...

Provincial legislature on Broadway.

PAM - Legislative Buildings Collection - N11777

Glimpses of the Way We Were

... but it was just a gatehouse for the real edifice, which opened in 1921.

Manitoba Legislature.

PAM - Legislative Buildings Collection - N16379

Winnipeg

THIS WAS a structure worthy of prairie dreamers! On top was the marvellous "Golden Boy," which every Manitoban believed to be a fairy tale symbol ...

Golden Boy being placed atop the Legislative Building.

PAM - Legislative Buildings Collection - N12129

Glimpses of the Way We Were

I WAS TAUGHT the "true" legend of the Golden Boy. It seems that King Henry I, the Norman they called "Beauclerc," who was the son of the murdered William Rufus, had only one legitimate son, William Atheling. He also had many rivals for the throne in both England and France. So, in 1120, he married Billy to the daughter of the King of France and sent him off to Paris in a beautiful new ship, called *The White Ship*. Also aboard was a solid gold statue, the Golden Boy, which was a present to the King of France. Alas, *The White Ship*, Prince William, and the Golden Boy were all lost in a storm at sea, thus planting the seeds of the Hundred Years War and the Wars of the Roses. Winnipeg's tie to this tale was a wonderfully romantic story — and one that was partially true. This version had *The White Ship*, Billy's bones, and the statue of the Golden Boy lying together at the bottom of the English Channel for seven hundred years. Finally, the story went, Louis Riel, or Lord Strathcona, or Sir Rodmond Roblin — one of those great Manitobans — went swimming in the Channel, discovered the statue, and brought it to Winnipeg just to crown our very own legislative building.

When I grew older I found out the truth: there *had* been a Prince William and a princess. There was even a *White Ship* and a shipwreck. But no Golden Boy. The statue on top of the Legislature had been commissioned by the Roblin government in 1912 and the sculptor was a Frenchman in Paris. The Golden Boy was not gold, but gold plated, and carried in its hand a wheat sheaf — the symbol of the west.

It was disillusioning to me: a boy grows up and finds there is no Santa Claus and no real Golden Boy ...

Still, when I was very young, I used to peer at the Golden Boy atop our greatest building, and shake my head in wonder!

The politicians were real enough, though ... Here are, in 1915, J.H. Ashdown, hardware tycoon and former mayor, and Premier T.C. Norris (who furnished the Legislature).

Winnipeg

Ashdown and Norris in an open automobile.

PAM - Foote Collection - N2520

Glimpses of the Way We Were

PREMIER NORRIS with his successor, John Bracken, when the latter was still a professor of agriculture ....

Bracken and Norris in a grain field in 1921.

PAM - Foote Collection - N2257

Winnipeg

J OHN BRACKEN himself, the leader of the Progressive Party, and the most successful politician in Manitoba history, at the radio microphone in 1925.

John Bracken in a radio studio.

PAM - Foote Collection - N1718

Glimpses of the Way We Were

Behind the politicians stood their maker and breaker, John Wesley Dafoe, editor of the *Free Press* for more than forty years, a towering national force in the Liberal Party.

John W. Dafoe in 1930.

PAM - N19450

Winnipeg

More important than Rodmond Roblin, T.C. Norris, and John Bracken combined was Nellie Mooney McClung, the woman who led the successful fight to bring the vote to women in 1916. She grew up on a farm in Manitoba's Souris Valley, became a schoolteacher, a novelist, and a leader of the suffragist movement. Her sharp Irish tongue and ease on a platform made every male politician squirm. Here she is in her fighting prime in 1910.

Nellie McClung.

PAM - N7694

Glimpses of the Way We Were

And here are her colleagues in 1915, presenting a petition for the women's vote.

Group of four suffragists.

PAM - Events Collection - N9905

Winnipeg

For all the frantic hustle of Winnipeg's building, the founders did a pretty good job of planning, and one of their great visions was public parks available to everyone. Right in the centre of town was tiny Central Park, sheltered under an awesome church. And the boulevards of Broadway were perfect for the spacious legislative grounds, the beginnings of the university, and the marble-faced law courts.

The planners and even the real estate operators made excellent use of the vast space available, spreading out along the winding banks of the two rivers.

Everybody went to Assiniboine Park for family gatherings, church picnics, cricket and tennis games, visits to the hothouse (no small thing in winter in a place as cold as Winnipeg!), strolls with your girl along the river, gawking at strange animals in the zoo. The first pavilion was a graceful, vaguely oriental structure. When it burned down the replacement had less charm at first, but its tower, like the tower of the old pavilion could be seen from anywhere in the park.

The old pavilion (1928).

PAM - Winnipeg Parks Collection - N31

Glimpses of the Way We Were

The new pavilion (1956).

PAM - Winnipeg Parks Collection - N4750

WINNIPEG

ANOTHER great asset to the city was Lake Winnipeg, located fifty or sixty miles to the north. The railways made access to the lake easier with spur lines to its beaches — the CPR to Winnipeg Beach in the west, and the CNR to Grand Beach in the east. Thousands of families rented tiny summer cottages within scampering distance of the lake. On summer Saturday nights there were "Moonlight Specials" to the big dance pavilion in Winnipeg Beach — the trains left at 6 p.m. and returned at midnight, with hundreds of happy couples necking on the dusty plush seats of the daycoaches.

Winnipeg Beach (1912).

PAM - Foote Collection - N2198

Glimpses of the Way We Were

Canoe racing at Lockport (1920).

PAM - Foote Collection - N2461

Winnipeg

Ah, but Winnipeg was most famous as the home of red-blooded team sports: baseball, rugby, hockey, curling, lacrosse!

Wesley College (now the University of Winnipeg) had a stadium right in the centre of the city and my dad took me to my first exhibition baseball there — a game between the Kansas City Monarchs (what was referred to as a "coloured" team in those days) and the bearded House of David team (white) from Benton Harbor, Michigan.

Everybody, amateur or pro, played at Wesley Stadium and there was a great debate in the 1930s when they put in electric lights for night games (but no artificial turf)!

Baseball in Wesley Stadium, 1920.

PAM - Foote Collection - N2654

Glimpses of the Way We Were

PEOPLE didn't start out needing a stadium, though. In 1891 they were playing rugby football on the bald prairie. The Winnipeg Blue Bombers came along half a century later and brought Winnipeg its first Grey Cup in 1935, when the immortal Fritz Hanson almost single-handedly defeated the Hamilton Tigers (not the Tiger-Cats then).

Rugby football (1891).

PAM - Sport Collection - N1496

Winnipeg

On the other hand, winter sports were more natural for Winnipeggers. Along with the vote, women were fighting for their place. Would you believe that as early as 1906 women were ... curling? Note the fashionable, athletically designed uniforms!

Women's curling teams.

PAM - Sport Collection - N1875

Glimpses of the Way We Were

River Park was not as fashionable as either Assiniboine or Kildonan parks, perhaps because this area, on both sides of the river, had long been settled by truck farmers. The permanent University of Manitoba was built nearby in the 1920s. But River Park itself became famous as an amusement park, noted for carnivals and side shows (whereas the big circuses were held in the North End). It was also great place for a winter carnival in 1924.

River Park Winter Carnival.

PAM - Foote Collection - N2640

WINNIPEG

Closer to the city, the Assiniboine River featured skating parties, just like those on the Rideau in Ottawa. Tent dressing rooms and everything.

Skating on the Assiniboine (1912).

PAM - Foote Collection - N2173

Glimpses of the Way We Were

WHAT WOULD any self-respecting metropolis be without the sport of kings? When I was a young reporter on the *Free Press*, there were two thoroughbred tracks and four meets a year — at Polo Park and Whittier Park. Every racing buff told of the young Winnipeg sports writer who joined Moe Annenberg's *Racing Form* and race wire and became the managing editor of Triangle Publications, which had termini in eight hundred pool rooms across the continent. It was so successful that Moe's son Walter became the publisher of the *Philadelphia Inquirer*, US ambassador to Britain, and one of the richest patrons of the arts in the world.

Here is Whittier Park in its 1925 heyday.

Whittier Park.

PAM - St. Boniface Parks Collection - N784

101

Winnipeg

WESLEY STADIUM was fine, but it was a bit small for Winnipeg in the 1920s, so Osborne Stadium was built near the downtown and next door to the great indoor rink and show centre, the Amphitheatre. The two facilities were across from the Legislature, at the corner of Broadway and Osborne, conveniently near the old Shea's brewery. Soon all the big hockey games were played at the Amphitheatre, while football and baseball were played at Osborne Stadium. The Blue Bombers met teams like the Calgary Stampeders and the Edmonton Eskimos there. I saw Lefty Grove of the Philadelphia Athletics, one of the greatest pitchers of all time, permanently injure his pitching arm at Osborne in an exhibition game after the World Series. It was so cold that day that he had to wear a jacket and gloves.
And, of course, there were track meets.

Osborne Stadium.

PAM - Winnipeg Buildings Collection - N15609

102

Glimpses of the Way We Were

... and Horse Shows.

The Amphitheatre (1912).

PAM - Winnipeg Buildings Collection

Winnipeg

But I am convinced God invented hockey with Winnipeg in mind! Why else would Winnipeg have a lock on junior and senior hockey from the 1920s to the 1950s? The Victorias started it all by winning the Stanley Cup in 1896 and 1901.

In 1920, the Falcons won the world championship at the Antwerp Olympics.

Winnipeg Falcons.

PAM - Sport Collection - N5476

Glimpses of the Way We Were

IN THE 1930s and 1940s, Winnipeg teams virtually owned the Memorial Cup for juniors. The Winnipeg Monarchs, the St. Boniface Seals, and the Winnipeg Rangers dominated the game until servicemen began to win the Allan Cup during the Second World War.

Winnipeg Monarchs, 1946-47.

PAM - Sport Collection - N3907

105

Winnipeg

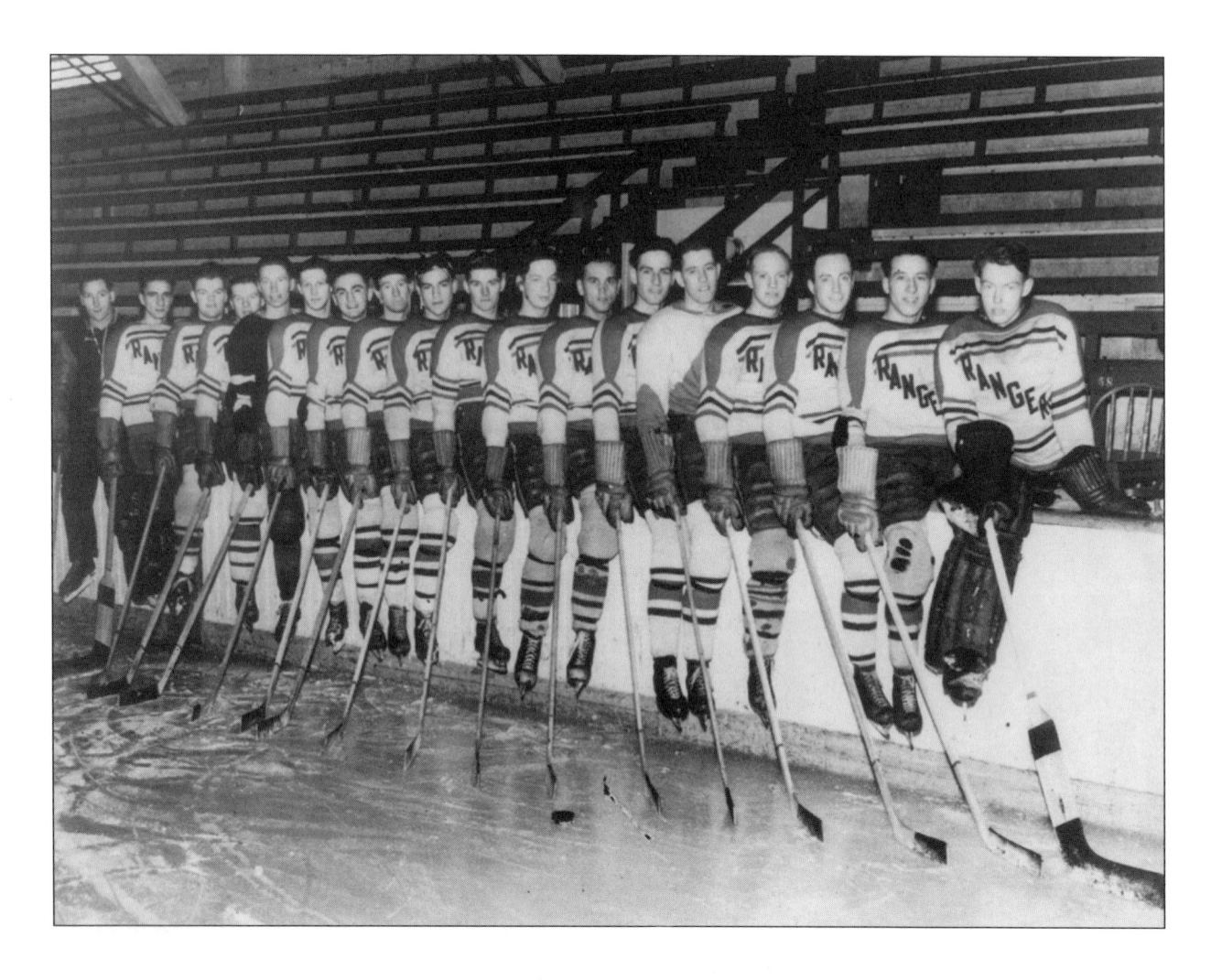

Winnipeg Rangers, 1941.

PAM - Sport Collection - N3907

Glimpses of the Way We Were

WINTER or summer, Winnipeggers knew how to enjoy themselves. There were band concerts in the bandstand at Central Park.

Central Park (1910).

PAM - Winnipeg Parks Collection - N15960

WINNIPEG

THOUSANDS packed the Lake Winnipeg beaches wearing the latest styles for bathing beauties ...

Crowds at Winnipeg Beach in 1912.

PAM - Foote Collection - N2198

Glimpses of the Way We Were

... while there were closeups of the ladies.

1915 styles were sexy.

PAM - Foote Collection - N2188

Winnipeg

Indoors, the local citizens were given a feast of entertainment. The Winnipeg Theatre was built in 1883, and was soon renamed Victoria Hall. C.P. Walker, an impresario from Fargo, North Dakota, made a $75,000 transformation of the Victoria into the splendidly reborn Winnipeg Theatre in 1896. This became the Winnipeg Opera House, and in 1904 Walker moved on to build the Walker Theatre, which stands to this very day. This theatre ranked with any in North America and brought to the West grand opera, concerts, the world's greatest soloists, plays, and pantomime.

Winnipeg Opera House (1900).

PAM - Winnipeg Theatres Collection

Glimpses of the Way We Were

ON A SLIGHTLY reduced scale was the Orpheum, which showed plays and superior movies. Of course, there were movie palaces everywhere, from elegant monsters on Portage to neighbourhood playhouses, where we kids watched serials every Saturday afternoon. The Province was famous for showing nothing but westerns.

The Orpheum (1911).

PAM - Winnipeg Theatres Collection - N10804

Winnipeg

The Province (1922).

PAM - Foote Collection - N2717

Glimpses of the Way We Were

With all this varied entertainment (plus circuses and carnivals) the greatest all-around entertainment came at church — especially in the Pentecostal Assembly's splendid Calvary Temple. It had started as a small neighourhood church with an intriguing sign: in big, electric letters were the words: "Jesus Saves!" and under them a small painted sign: "Every night but Thursday."

The church grew and prospered and finally bought a huge, red-brick Baptist church in the heart of town — Calvary Temple.

In my years on the *Free Press*, it was the best all-around show in Winnipeg, supplying the faithful with visiting evangelists, two orchestras, four choirs, a syncopated quartet, and a pipe organ. The pastor played the slide trombone; his father, another evangelist, played a jazzy cornet; his mother a hot piano, and his sister a soaring clarinet.

The pastor in my time was a tall, good-looking orator who led the choirs in hymn-singing contests while the orchestras accompanied the voices of the congregation. There were singing contests between the congregation in the nave and the congregation in the balcony, between men and women, and between young and old.

But wonderfully staged drama was the specialty of the church.

When the congregation was ready, the lights slowly dimmed and were replaced by the white beams of a vast cross above the pulpit. When it was fully lit, the congregation was blinded by the light. And as the light of the cross came up, for the first time the pipe organ rose from a whisper to a thunder of hypnotic frenzy. Sinners, guided and encouraged by well-trained ushers, stumbled down the aisles to the penitents' benches crying "Hallelujah!" and gabbling "in tongues." It was magnificent theatre, surpassing any Shakespearean company a few blocks away at the Walker Theatre.

WINNIPEG

Calvary Temple.

Calvary Temple Archives

Glimpses of the Way We Were

O N A far more elitist level, the rich (including the Siftons, who owned the *Free Press*) "rode to hounds" in Charleswood ...

"Riding to Hounds" (1912).

PAM - Foote Collection - N2082

Winnipeg

Perhaps the most dramatic event in Winnipeg history was the General Strike in 1919. The Great War was scarcely over and thousands of soldiers had returned home. The Russian Revolution had occurred and the Bolsheviks were being invaded by several allied armies. Every other country feared the spread of revolution, but the radical elements were strong in Winnipeg, where there was a large garment industry. Even policemen were seeking union recognition. The unions went out in sympathy with a telephone operators' strike in Seattle, and the middle and wealthy classes established a "Committee of 1,000," which manned the trolley cars and backed up the militia and the police. On the other side there were clergymen-turned-social-workers like J.S. Woodsworth, later a distinguished member of the federal Parliament and founder of the Cooperative Commonwealth Federation. There were riots, and tanks and machine guns were used. A non-striker was killed. Some strike leaders went to jail, others were deported. The strike lasted for weeks, and though it was finally broken, it led to stronger unions in the end.

Police holding Main Street after a riot in the 1919 General Strike.

PAM - Foote Collection - N2764

Glimpses of the Way We Were

Confrontation.

PAM - Foote Collection - N2758

Winnipeg

Returning veterans demonstrate.

PAM - Winnipeg Strike Collection - N12295

Glimpses of the Way We Were

WINNIPEG'S DEPENDENCE on the railways and river systems was supplemented by the airplane in the 1920s. Flown by daring young men who had fought the Red Baron in the Great War in tiny fighter biplanes, the bush plane became the key to northern Canada. The planes were equipped with wheels, skis, or pontoons, depending on the season or terrain, and could land anywhere, most of the year (except during freeze up and breakup). The pilots flew as far as the Arctic Ocean, and the Winnipeg and Edmonton airports were the gateways to the north as well as filling stations for transcontinental airliners. The glamour flights were in the north, where daring young men in their flying machines took off regularly in Flin Flon and The Pas and Aklavik and Churchill.

I remember seeing a couple of paragraphs on the front page of the *Free Press*: Wop May, the legendary bush pilot, had brought a prospector back from Norway House. Taking off in the bush, his right ski had caught in a root, and when he arrived at Stevenson Field one ski was hanging at a right angle. The control tower saw it and wigwagged him off. His passenger looked out the door and saw what had happened. Wop asked him to get out and stand on the back end of the ski, hanging on to a wing strut. That brought the ski back level and that was the way they landed.

It rated no more than a couple of paragraphs in the paper.

May, Leigh Brintnell, Punch Dickins, and Grant McConachie were the men who opened up the Canadian north. Here F.J. Stevenson, for whom the Winnipeg airport is named, flies newspapers to Red Lake in 1927.

F.J. Stevenson flying north.

PAM - C.A.L. Collection - 1665

Winnipeg

From 1920 on, the northern outposts were supplied by air, and the pioneer "flying boxcar" was the Junkers low-winged monoplane, great-granddaddy of the Hercules Transport and the Globemaster. Here is the Junkers in 1932, picking up cargo on the Assiniboine River.

Junkers freighter on floats.

PAM - C.A.L. Collection - 952

Glimpses of the Way We Were

ONE OF WINNIPEG'S greatest institutions was the daily newspaper, and in its heyday there were three: the *Manitoba Free Press*, the *Tribune*, and the *Telegram*. Of these, the greatest was the *Free Press*, which was Clifford Sifton's mighty voice in bringing the hundreds of thousands of immigrants to the West. Sifton was Interior Minister in Laurier's "cabinet of many talents" in 1896, and his editor, even more powerful than himself, was John W. Dafoe. Clifford Sifton left Laurier's cabinet in 1911 over reciprocity with the United States, but Dafoe stayed with the government and took the newspaper with him — something almost unheard of in publishing. Until he died in 1944, Dafoe was the true editorial voice of the *Free Press*, even though the Sifton family had long resumed financial control.

In 1912, the Manitoba Free Press *(right) nuzzled up to the imposing Post Office on Portage Avenue.*

PAM - Winnipeg Buildings Collection - N7956

Winnipeg

THE *TRIBUNE* and the *Telegram* never reached the popularity of the *Free Press*, partly because the *Free Press* owned the weekly *Prairie Farmer*, which was the Bible for farmers across the West. The *Telegram* had a reputation of being a mouthpiece of the Tory party, while the *Tribune* never touched the broader prairie elements. The *Free Press* dominated the scene the way the *Des Moines Register* did Iowa.

The Winnipeg Free Press's *new building on Carlton, off Portage. (1936).*

PAM - Winnipeg Buildings Collection - N721

Glimpses of the Way We Were

The 1910 staff of the Winnipeg Tribune.

PAM - Winnipeg Buildings Collection - N17227

WINNIPEG

The Telegram *(1903).*

PAM - Outsize Collection - N1551

124

Glimpses of the Way We Were

The Telegram's *crowded city room (1916).*

PAM - Foote Collection - N2354

WINNIPEG

I STARTED WORK on the *Winnipeg Free Press* in the Carlton Street building one week before the Second World War started. The *Telegram* had long been gone; the *Tribune* was fighting hard to compete. We felt we were in a battle as fierce as those between Hearst and Pulitzer in New York in 1900, though the owners of the two newspapers made all kinds of arrangements between themselves.

The *Free Press* was Liberal politically but not socially. The word "rape" never was used in its pages — victims were "assaulted." Many subjects were never covered. The private lives of politicians were decently ignored, unless the politicians were so unfortunate as to wind up in court, in which case legal testimony was carried at length. There was one Ukrainian reporter who covered nothing but Ukrainian social news. All Christian church events were covered lavishly, though the church editor, a meek little man, was famous for writing erotic fiction in his spare time. At first there were no Jewish reporters, although the wealthy Jewish institutions were given coverage.

Women were a different matter. When it came to hiring women, the *Free Press* was ahead of its time. Its expert on crops for forty years was the legendary E. Cora Hinde, who was respected more than the insurance companies or the government experts for her crop predictions. The "slot boss" (copy chief) of the news desk was Louise ("Louie") McDonald, a former city hall reporter. Many women, like Barbara Chipman Kilvert, Virginia Cameron Russell, Olive Dickason, Ann Phelps, and Heather Robertson got their start at the *Free Press*.

We were all clones of the characters in *The Front Page*, that satirical record of Chicago in the 1920s written by Ben Hecht and Charles MacArthur. Every cub religiously read "City Editor" by Stanley Walker, legendary city editor of the *New York Herald Tribune*, and we all competed to cover murder investigations and trials. Jimmy Gray, the dapper city hall reporter in my day, later wrote the best histories of Winnipeg that have been printed. Steve Wilson and Stan Bentham were the very epitome of police reporters in Chicago.

There were also a number of colourful drifters who inhabited the news room late at night and used idle typewriters, telephones, and *Free Press* copy paper: Freddie Palmer, the defrocked alderman; "Bald-headed Bobby," the wordy anarchist; Jim Wright, who wrote a prize-winning history of the Doukhobors on our typewriters (he won a 50,000 ruble Stalin Prize for Literature but couldn't collect it because of the hot war and then the cold war); and Jeanie, the sweet, crazy bag lady.

I personally got to know a little man who came in regularly to collect the Chinese world news. I gathered bundles of wire-service copy and he translated the relevant parts into Chinese and posted them on a wall in Chinatown.

Such are my memories of growing to manhood on a great, Winnipeg newspaper.

All that time the city was growing, building, and tearing down through boom and bust, several wars, many governments ...

Glimpses of the Way We Were

High shot of streetcar tracks being repaired along Portage Avenue. Wesley College is at centre, left; Hudson's Bay Company store is at top, right (1930).

PAM - Foote Collection N2707

Winnipeg

The Fort Garry Hotel, centre; Main Street Bridge, foreground (1931).

PAM - Foote Collection - N2267

Glimpses of the Way We Were

Aerial panorama (1950).

PAM - Winnipeg Views Collection - N8439

WINNIPEG

... floods came and went. The worst in history had driven George Simpson and the Hudson's Bay Company from the Forks to Lower Fort Garry. In 1916, pedestrians had to cross by footbridge from St. Boniface to Winnipeg. And in 1950, facing the worst floods since 1826, nuns at St. Mary's Academy faced the world cheerfully from a canoe overlooking the posh, underwater homes of Wellington Crescent.

Footbridge from St. Boniface.

PAM - Floods Collection - N13361

Nuns in a canoe.

PAM - Floods Collection - N16103

Glimpses of the Way We Were

WINNIPEG EVEN INSPIRED one of the great books for children — A.A. Milne's *Winnie the Pooh*. In 1914, Captain Harry Colebourn, bound for overseas service, acquired a bear cub as a mascot which he named "Winnie" (for his native Winnipeg). It ended up in the London Zoo where A.A. Milne and his son, Christopher Robin, discovered it and wrote it into history. A Winnipeg legend to go with the Golden Boy atop the Legislative Building!

THE WONDER OF WINNIPEG is that it became a fully modern, dynamic, and well-rounded city of 100,000 people in less than one generation. Those false-front shacks on Main Street were replaced by brick-and-stone ornaments to Victorian civilization in twenty years. Space planning was superb, and though there was no town planning in the modern sense, the office buildings, factories, warehouses, and public edifices were triumphs of idiosyncrasy — every budding millionaire was building his own pyramid to last into infinity. Many of these buildings survive today, nestled among the immense skyscrapers which are the monuments of the second half of the twentieth century.

Nevertheless, in the end, Winnipeg comes back to the people who rushed in from all over the world to create a new Camelot — the stalwart immigrant families romanticized by Sir Clifford Sifton when he was the minister responsible for bringing them in ...

Captain Harry Colebourn with "Winnie the Pooh."

PAM - D. Harry Colebourn Collection

PAM - Foote Collection - N2064